Neighbours
ANNUAL 1989

£3.95

Neighbours ANNUAL 1989

CONTENTS

© 1988 World International Publishing Ltd.
All rights reserved.
Published in Great Britain by
World International Publishing Ltd.,
an Egmont Company, Egmont House,
P.O. Box 111, 61 Great Ducie Street,
Manchester M60 3BL.
Printed in Italy. ISBN 7235 6841 3

Picture Credits
London Features International Ltd: *5, 7, 8, 18, 27, 36, 40, 42, 52, 53, 54, 58*
Pictorial Press Limited: *12, 14, 15, 18, 32, 35, 53*
Scope Features: *7, 9, 10, 16, 22, 29, 37, 46, 48, 50, 51*
Syndication International (1986) Ltd: *13, 14, 21, 23, 26, 28, 37, 38, 44, 45, 46, 56, 58, 59*
The Royal Greenwich Observatory: *19*
Topham Picture Library: *30, 33*
Cover Photos by Pictorial Press Ltd & Scope Features

This is an independent publication, unconnected with any particular artist or management group.

The **NEIGHBOURS** Annual is written by Brenda Apsley, Clive Hopwood & Nick Pemberton.

ONLY A FOOTSTEP AWAY

A few years ago nobody could have questioned the undoubted supremacy of *Coronation Street* as Britain's No. 1 soap, a position it held almost as of right. Rivals came and went, or ambled along in its shadow, content with vastly inferior viewing figures.

Then along came *EastEnders* and suddenly the Street was no longer at the top. **Neighbours** was never intended as a rival, having been bought in as a cheap daytime soap by the BBC, but...

Little did they know that **Neighbours** mania was going to break out all over Britain. Once it was rescheduled to show at lunchtime and early evening the programme really began to take off.

Almost overnight viewing figures doubled, and then kept climbing, overtaking the Street, breathing down the neck of the residents of Albert Square. Now, more people in Britain watch **Neighbours** each day than the entire population of Australia!

Visiting stars from the soap draw enormous crowds wherever they go, and the craze has begun to spread throughout Europe. America, Africa and the Far East are next. The dedicated fans, of course, always knew the soap from Down Under would come out on top.

And now — the very first **Neighbours** annual, packed with photos and features of your favourite soap. By the time you read this annual, who knows, **Neighbours** may have tipped *EastEnders* from the top spot. They are, after all, only a footstep away from becoming the No. 1 show in the UK!

Meet the

RAMSAY

WELCOME TO THE MOST FAMOUS STREET IN AUSTRALIA, RAMSAY STREET. The regular fans of BBC's twice daily Aussie import will need no introduction to the famous families whose daily lives keep 15 million people glued to their TV screens (that's more than the whole population of Australia!).

But for those of you who have been living on another planet for the last couple of years, or anyone who might be in need of a quick refresher course, here's a brief introduction to those friends and neighbours from Down Under. But first...

RAMSAY STREET

A middle class suburb, like many in Australia's great cities, the Ramsay Street area still has some surviving signs of its distant past. One or two settlers' houses still stand, although rather the worse for wear these days, and you can still find the odd orchard or market garden which was the area's first foundation of prosperity.

Nowadays it is very much a suburb of the 80s. It has a railway, pleasant tree-lined streets, a shopping mall, and all the usual amenities – schools and churches, a pub, post office, community centre and library, and a retirement centre for senior citizens.

Jack Ramsay was an original settler, serving on the local council for almost fifty years, twice as mayor. His family still lives there...

"Ramsay Street is a very long street and we intend to move gradually along it" Reg Watson

6

Neighbours of

STREET

MADGE MITCHELL – Shane's aunt, and these days the centre of the Ramsay household after the departure of her brother Max and his estranged wife, Maria. Voted 'Mum of the Year' in Australia, Madge may have a hard edge to her, but underneath there's a good heart.

SHANE – no longer resident in the street, but a firm favourite with viewers for his good looks and physique! (BBC viewers still have the chance to view actor Peter O'Brien in the recently imported Aussie series *The Flying Doctors*.) His career as an Olympic diver cut short by a car accident, Shane was very much the street's Romeo.

CHARLENE MITCHELL – Madge's daughter, and the cause of much anguish to her mother. Unsettled by her parents' divorce she finally seems to be settling down to her new life, especially now she's heading down the aisle with Scott Robinson.

Meet the

RAMSAY

JIM – the mature love interest in the street, he has brought up his family after the death of his wife shortly after she gave birth to their youngest, Lucy. A level-headed, caring man whose first concern is for his children.

PAUL – a young man rather wrapped up in the family business after a disastrous marriage to Terry ended in his wife being jailed for attempted murder. Her subsequent suicide only made Paul withdraw even further into himself. The question for viewers is whether the right woman will come along to bring him out of himself – and hold on to him.

SCOTT – pin-up for teenagers, Scott kept everyone guessing with his on-off relationship with Charlene. A good and understanding relationship with his father – apart from the usual occasional teenage hiccup – has made him into a likeable, hard working young man. There's many a young viewer who envies Charlene!

LUCY – the baby of the family who's adapted well to having lost her mother at such an early age. A bit of a tomboy, she's adopted her grandmother as a substitute mum.

HELEN DANIELS – Lucy's grandmother, who stepped in to help when Jim's wife died. A cool-headed businesswoman, she's the one most people turn to when they want sensible, practical advice on serious matters.

"It's hard being a sole parent"
Alan Dale on Jim Robinson

Neighbours of

STREET

AND THEN THERE'S...

DES CLARKE – bank manager who after an inauspicious early romantic career landed the pick of the crop when Daphne jilted Shane at the altar. His formidable mother, EILEEN, played the matchmaker.

DAPHNE CLARKE – ex-stripper who moved into Ramsay Street as a lodger, nearly got married to Shane, and in the end plumped for solidly reliable Des. Her dramatic exit from the street had viewers reaching for the paper hankies.

CLIVE GIBBONS – not exactly the village idiot, being a qualified doctor, but certainly the funster in Ramsay Street. (He proposed to Susan dressed as a clown!) Life was never dull when Clive was around.

MIKE YOUNG – Scott's best mate. A troubled family background doesn't seem to have stopped Mike turning out as a genuinely nice guy...with a body to match (hardly surprising since actor Guy Pearce is a fitness fanatic).

"If I met her in real life I'd probably be very rude to her"
Vivean Gray on Mrs Mangel

MRS MANGEL – the street gossip, always with a bad word for the 'youth of today' and generally guaranteed to stir anything that hasn't already been thoroughly shaken. Like Ena Sharples from the early days of *Coronation Street*, one of the viewers' favourites. You can always expect a bit of action when Mrs Mangel gets in on the act!

9

 **STAR**

PROFILE

10

KYLIE MINOGUE

alias CHARLENE MITCHELL

ON HER EARLY LIFE

"I was born in 1968, in Bethlehem actually! Bethlehem Hospital in Melbourne. I've got one brother, Brendan, who's eighteen, and a sister, Danielle, who's sixteen."

ON HER EARLY CAREER

"I got my first acting job when I was eleven and in grade six. I was in one episode of *Skyways*. Jason was in it too. He played my brother. After that I was in *The Sullivans* for a while. After that, I didn't do anything till 1984."

ON HER ROLE AS CHARLENE

"My face fitted the part and everything took off. There is a bit of me in Charlene, but I don't fight with my mother like she does. I think viewers like Charlene because she's an average teenager growing up and having difficulties. I worry sometimes that viewers will identify with her character too much. I don't want seventeen year olds leaving home to get married like Charlene did. It would be on my conscience. When Charlene's being irresponsible and a tomboy, she's not like me at all!"

ON THE PRESSURES OF THE SHOW

"I work a twelve hour day on **Neighbours** starting at six thirty in the morning. I'm in the studio from six forty five till seven fifteen in the evening. And even when you're not in front of the cameras you have to spend the rest of the day waiting in the dark and smoky green room."

"It can be a very lonely life"

KYLIE MINOGUE

ON FAME

"At the risk of sounding sorry for myself, it can be a very lonely life. I envy other people of my age sometimes. Most nineteen year olds don't have a care in the world, and I wonder if it's all been worth the price. Sometimes I feel lonely when there are so many people around who want me to do things and I can't let them down. I get home, and I've got no time to myself. I can't get out and enjoy myself much. I know it's a corny complaint but you do get too well known to sit and have a good time in a restaurant or go dancing in a nightclub. You DO become public property. It's not the kind of atmosphere to meet Mr Right."

ON HER CO-STAR JASON DONOVAN

"We spent Christmas together in Tahiti. It was the most fantastic week of my life. It was wonderful. Sometimes I don't know what I'd do without Jason. We've known each other since we were eleven and get on better every day. Jason is part of my life. It's fantastic to be with someone who's going through the same sort of problems and understands the pressures you're under."

ON THE FUTURE

"One day I'd like to lead a normal life and not be nagged by people about losing too much weight. Sometimes I do wish I just had a nine to five job. I think about all the people out there breaking their necks to become actresses or singers and I feel sure my luck won't last. I miss having girlfriends and things like that, but I know that if I don't concentrate on my careers now, I may never get another chance."

"I envy other people of my own age sometimes"

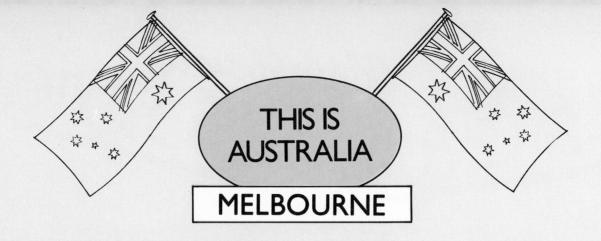

THIS IS AUSTRALIA

MELBOURNE

Today, Melbourne is the second city in Australia, capital of the state of Victoria and home to some three million people. It is a thriving commercial centre, and its factories produce aircraft, cars and textiles. It houses vast food processing plants, and Melbourne's port handles many ships from all over the world.

But it was all very different back in 1802. Then, the area at the mouth of the Yarra River was peopled by Aborigines. It was named Port Phillip Bay by Lieutenent John Murray, an English explorer and commander of the *Lady Nelson*, when he sailed into the huge natural harbour.

Some years before, settlements had been set up successfully on the island of Van Diemen's Land (now Tasmania), and by 1834 the pioneers had heard much about the rich country of the southern mainland from whalers and seal traders. Seeking new grazing lands, a settler called John Batman sailed across the Bass Strait in 1835 and built a house in the Port Phillip area. He hoped that one day the settlement might grow to be a village...

He could not have foreseen the area's thriving future. Settlers arrived to trade and work the land, and the settlement grew and grew. In the 1850s gold was discovered in Victoria, and many more people arrived to live in the area. The settlement grew from one house...to village...to town...and to the great city of Melbourne as we know it today.

Unlike the settlers in the rest of Australia, John Batman did not just take the land from the Aborigines who lived there; he 'bought' it. The price for the many square kilometres?
20 pairs of blankets
12 tomahawks
10 looking glasses
30 knives
12 pairs of scissors
12 red shirts
50 pounds of flour
4 suits of clothes
50 handkerchiefs

Neighbours SCRAP BOOK

Neighbours is watched by an estimated five million Australians daily – almost one third of the country's population.

Having heard that he was a fan of the show, **Neighbours** producers asked British pop star George Michael if he would like to make a guest appearance as a DJ, early last year. George, however, who was in the middle of a series of concert dates Down Under, had to turn the offer down as he was "too busy".

Kylie Minogue's earliest memory is of a pair of boots she owned whilst in kindergarten. "I thought they were so trendy," she says. "They were white vinyl with a round toe and a zipper on the side and a black smile on the front of them! That's about as far back as I go."

The late Myra de Groot, who played Des' mother Eileen until her death last year, once described her on-screen character as being "mad as a meat axe".

Neighbours can even count royalty amongst its followers. During her visit to Australia to participate in the nation's bi-centenary celebrations, Princess Diana was introduced to Kylie Minogue after a rock concert. The Princess confessed to being a fan of the show and said that she couldn't wait to get home and catch up on what she had missed.

Peter O'Brien was on a beach near Sydney teaching schoolchildren to surf when he learned that he had landed the role of Shane in **Neighbours**.

A single half hour episode of **Neighbours** costs £20,000 to produce – slightly less than half what it costs the BBC to produce an episode of *EastEnders*.

Neighbours SCRAP BOOK

Peter O'Brien and Elaine Smith, whose failed romance in Neighbours succeeded in real life, have certainly made Britain their second home. Although neither are now in **Neighbours** in Australia, they are still very much among the most popular stars in the UK. So much so, that they have been tempted into British theatre. Scottish-born Elaine completed a series of plays for the Melbourne Theatre Company before joining Peter, during a five-month break from his role in *The Flying Doctors*. They teamed up to star in *Butterflies Are Free*, a Broadway hit from the sixties, which did a 10 week UK tour. After that it was straight into panto with *Mother Goose* at the Davenport Theatre in Stockport. As for future plans, Peter's made it clear he wouldn't say no to a part in *EastEnders*...now that's a ripper of an idea, Shane! Look out, Den, here comes Crocodile O'Brien...

Meanwhile...Kylie Minogue, Jason Donovan and Charlene Fenn have also signed up for panto, too: Kylie as Aladdin, Jason as Prince Charming (what else?) and Charlene as Cinderella. Hope they've remembered to pack their winter woollies; Christmas in Melbourne is usually up in the 70's fahrenheit (that's 20°C), so they'll notice a difference!

Peter O'Brien's new role as pilot Sam Patterson is somewhat out of character: he's scared of flying! "I tend to get paranoid, especially in big jets," he confesses. "I've had a lot of bad luck on some flights and I guess I've just lost my nerve." Luckily for Peter he never has to leave the ground during filming.

 **STAR**

PROFILE

JASON DONOVAN
alias SCOTT ROBINSON

"Dad warned me not to become an actor"

ON HIS EARLY LIFE
"I only saw Mum on Christmas and birthdays, and then not always. Dad and I were by ourselves from the time I was five until I was twelve, which are pretty important years. A lot of the time it was pretty rough on Dad and we became very close. And when my dad remarried when I was fifteen, Mum cut contact with me completely. I never see nor hear from her now – not even a birthday card."

ON LIFE IN AUSTRALIAN SOAPS
"Dad is an actor so during the time that Dad and I were alone, before he remarried, I spent plenty of time on film and TV locations. It's not as if it was something that I knew nothing about. There's just something about it when you've been around it like I have that's irresistible.

"Dad warned me not to become an actor, because the business was so unstable. Believe me, I'm aware that all this could end tomorrow."

ON HIS ROLE AS SCOTT
"I've done most of the things Scott's done – school exams and things like that – so I don't really have to go too far to understand his character."

ON CRITICISM
"Some people can't help it. They tell you that you're only there because your dad is a big TV actor. You get a lot of digs when you're in the public eye."

"I'm aware this could all end tomorrow"

17

JASON DONOVAN

ON FAME

"When I go out with my friends it can be embarrassing when people come up to me. But all my friends think it's really funny. I suppose it's all part of the business, and you'd be lying if you said that you didn't enjoy it."

"Not all my fan mail is from girls. One guy sent a picture of himself standing next to a Ferrari. He described himself in pretty intimate detail and wanted me to meet him at a certain time and place. I didn't go!"

ON HIS FRIENDSHIP WITH CO-STAR KYLIE MINOGUE

"Because we're a couple on-screen, people want to label us a couple off-screen as well. I don't see why people can't understand that we can be friends without having a relationship. That's all we are, purely friends."

ON MARRIAGE

"A certain amount of what your parents do rubs off on you. It's certainly made me think twice about marriage. I guess a separation can make you pretty independent. I have always done my own washing and can cook up quite an omelette."

ON THE FUTURE

"I'm only nineteen. I've got a lot of things to do and I don't really want to be tied down."

THIS IS AUSTRALIA

TERRA INCOGNITA

Ptolemy was one of the greatest geographers of ancient times. In AD 150 he wrote of a land he believed to be in the extreme south of the world, joining Asia to Africa. He called it *Terra Australis Incognita* — the unknown southern land.

For more than a thousand years the country we now call Australia remained the unknown land — unknown to the white man, but not to those who had already found it: the Aborigines.

They had travelled across the seas by boat from Java and other islands and lived in the vast country for many thousands of years. They lived a wandering, nomadic life, living in the open without shelter, roaming in groups in search of new hunting grounds and water. Their simple lifestyle changed forever with the arrival of the first white men...

We cannot be certain about which Europeans actually discovered Australia, but it is possible that the Portuguese reached it in the 1500s. A Spaniard called Luis Vaez de Torres gave an account of some 'very large islands' in 1606; they were, in fact, the hills of Cape York, the northernmost tip of Australia.

Abel Tasman and other Dutch explorers visited Australia in the years that followed, naming the land New Holland, but in 1770 Captain James Cook landed at Botany Bay on 29th April, and claimed the land for Britain.

His arrival, and the first penal colony set up eighteen years later, signalled the beginnings of Australia as we know it today. It was no longer the unknown land...

Way back in 1985, a quietly spoken Queenslander by the name of Reg Watson had an idea. Reg had been the producer of ITV's *Crossroads* here in Britain during the late sixties. He had spent most of the seventies back home in his native land working for the Grundy Corporation, Australia's largest producer of television shows, where he had been responsible for such programmes as *The Young Doctors*, *Sons and Daughters*, *Prisoner: Cell Block H*, and many more.

SIMPLICITY

Reg Watson's idea was simple. "I wanted to show three families living in a small street in a Melbourne suburb, who are friends," he now explains. "Humour was to play a big part in it and the other important thing was to show young people communicating with older people. In fact, the format was hard to get right because of its simplicity. I wrote the first episode of **Neighbours** twenty times before it felt right."

Low ratings caused cancellation

Crossroads

Reg worked on the show with producer John Holmes of the Seven Network, and the show was first broadcast by that organization in 1985. However, the show wasn't an instant success. Peter Pinne, Grundy's vice president, says: "Channel Seven was also showing *A Country Practice* and *Sons and Daughters*. They couldn't sustain all three." The show's afternoon time slot didn't help its ratings either, and after 171 episodes, **Neighbours** was cancelled.

But the **Neighbours** viewers, though not large in number, were fierce in their loyalty, and the Grundy Organization was besieged with mail demanding the return of their favourites. Eventually the chairman of Grundy took the show to Channel Ten, an unprecedented move, who took it up. Says Peter Pinne, "Channel Seven were so outraged we're told that they burned all the **Neighbours** sets. Eventually Channel Ten put it out early evening with redesigned sets and good publicity and an early evening time slot — and here we are."

"The format was very hard to get right because of its simplicity"

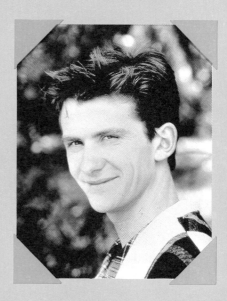

NEW FACES

In the change between channels the show lost some old faces and gained some new ones. Max Ramsay, the loudmouthed plumber, disappeared when actor Francis Bell refused his new contract. Writers substituted a brother, Tom Ramsay, to take his place. Darius Perkins, who had originally played the role of Scott Robinson had, by his own admission, become too difficult to work with, and his part was taken over by Jason Donovan. There were some protests from viewers

at first, but it wasn't long before Jason had stamped the role as his own.

However, the two most important new additions to the show were Madge Mitchell (Anne Charleston) and her daughter, Charlene (Kylie Minogue). Soon Kylie and Jason had become, at least for **Neighbours**' younger fans, the stars of the show. The show itself, within a space of a single year since its first broadcast on Channel Ten in January of 1986, had risen to become one of the nation's top television programmes, watched regularly by more than five million people.

Protest from viewers

Michael Grade took daughter's advice

NEIGHBOURS UK

It was at this point that the BBC bought the show from Channel Ten. Like other Australian soaps it was considered at first as daytime fodder, watched by an audience of housewives, shiftworkers, and the unemployed, but unable to hold its own against such homegrown products as *EastEnders* and *Coronation Street*. Nonetheless, the show had soon established a healthy enough viewing audience of around six million.

It was then that Michael Grade, at that time the Controller of BBC1, had a most revealing conversation with his daughter Alison. The sixteen year old told her father that she and her schoolfriends watched the show as often as they could by sneaking into the school's computer room. Mr Grade, realizing there was an as yet untapped audience for the show amongst the nation's schoolchildren, decided to show the programme twice a day, once at lunchtime, and then once again in the early evening.

NEVER ENDING STORY

This was done in January 1988, and within the space of one month the show's audience had more than doubled, making it the third most popular show on British television and turning its youthful cast into international stars almost overnight. **Neighbours**mania was well and truly here!

But can the show's popularity last? Critics of the show say that already the storylines are getting stretched – after all, there's only a certain number of permutations that the members of the cast can go through. But Reg Watson, the man who made it all happen in the first place, isn't too worried about that. "Ramsay Street is a very long street," he says, "and we intend to move gradually along it."

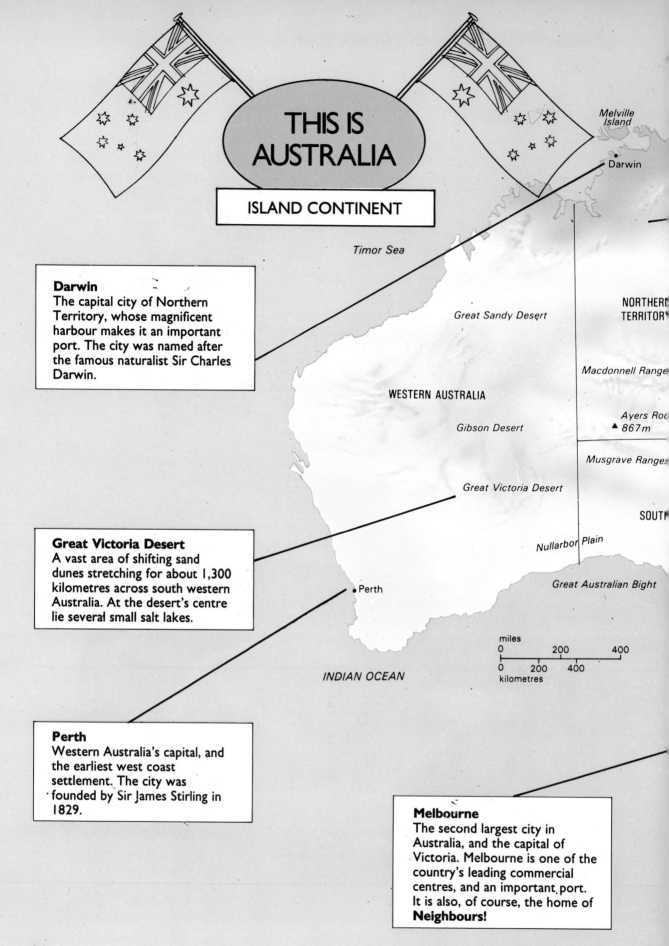

THIS IS AUSTRALIA

ISLAND CONTINENT

Darwin
The capital city of Northern Territory, whose magnificent harbour makes it an important port. The city was named after the famous naturalist Sir Charles Darwin.

Great Victoria Desert
A vast area of shifting sand dunes stretching for about 1,300 kilometres across south western Australia. At the desert's centre lie several small salt lakes.

Perth
Western Australia's capital, and the earliest west coast settlement. The city was founded by Sir James Stirling in 1829.

Melbourne
The second largest city in Australia, and the capital of Victoria. Melbourne is one of the country's leading commercial centres, and an important port. It is also, of course, the home of **Neighbours!**

Melville Island

Darwin

Timor Sea

Great Sandy Desert

NORTHERN TERRITORY

WESTERN AUSTRALIA

Macdonnell Range

Gibson Desert

Ayers Rock
▲ 867m

Musgrave Ranges

Great Victoria Desert

SOUTH

Nullarbor Plain

Great Australian Bight

• Perth

miles
0   200   400

0   200   400
kilometres

INDIAN OCEAN

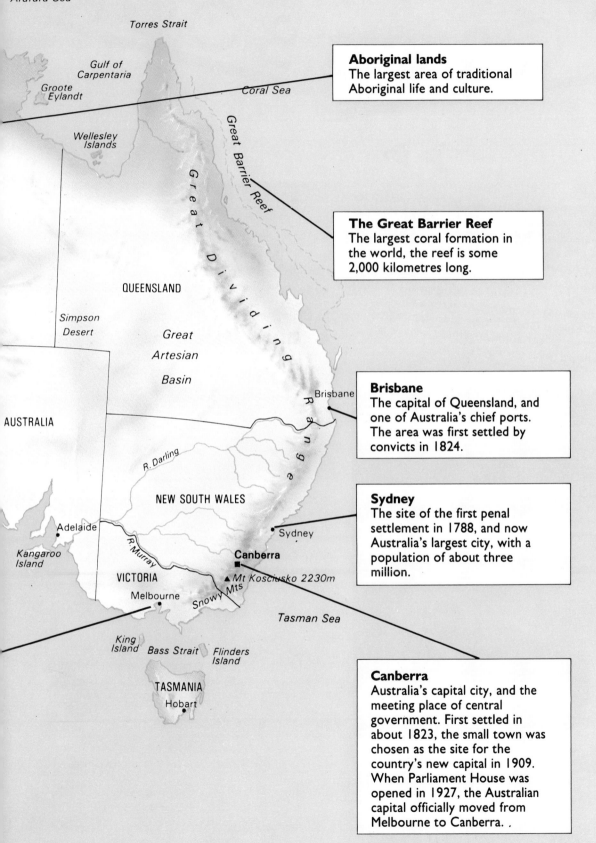

Arafura Sea

Torres Strait

Gulf of Carpentaria

Groote Eylandt

Coral Sea

Aboriginal lands
The largest area of traditional Aboriginal life and culture.

Wellesley Islands

Great Barrier Reef

Great Dividing Range

The Great Barrier Reef
The largest coral formation in the world, the reef is some 2,000 kilometres long.

QUEENSLAND

Simpson Desert

Great Artesian Basin

Brisbane

Brisbane
The capital of Queensland, and one of Australia's chief ports. The area was first settled by convicts in 1824.

AUSTRALIA

R. Darling

NEW SOUTH WALES

Sydney
The site of the first penal settlement in 1788, and now Australia's largest city, with a population of about three million.

Adelaide

R. Murray

Sydney

Canberra

Kangaroo Island

▲ Mt Kosciusko 2230m

VICTORIA

Melbourne

Snowy Mts

Tasman Sea

King Island

Bass Strait

Flinders Island

Canberra
Australia's capital city, and the meeting place of central government. First settled in about 1823, the small town was chosen as the site for the country's new capital in 1909. When Parliament House was opened in 1927, the Australian capital officially moved from Melbourne to Canberra. .

TASMANIA

Hobart

Home for Peter O'Brien was once a seminary for an order of monks. The building had fallen into disrepair when Peter and a bunch of mates took it over. "It was practically falling down," says the former **Neighbours** star. However, Peter and his friends rebuilt the place from top to bottom. "Now there are eight of us living here – five girls and three boys – and not an actor amongst them! I know most of these kids from school. When we all get home together we have an instant party on our hands."

Kylie Minogue attributes the largest part of her chart success not to her own talents as a singer, but to her producers Stock, Aitken and Waterman. "I don't think you have to be a really fabulous singer for them to give you a hit. They really know what they are doing and you are just a part of it," she says.

The name Kylie comes from an Aborigine word for a boomerang.

Alan Dale who plays the role of Jim Robinson once had the job of a milkman in his native New Zealand.

When Peter O'Brien was flying across the continent to take part in a charity appeal he had his first class ticket downgraded to second and the difference donated to the appeal. "Well, I mean it's only me," he explained. "There's really no need to make a fuss."

Neighbours
SCRAPBOOK

Author Robert Treborlang reckons **Neighbours** is not quite the whole truth. In his book *No Worries: How To Survive Australians*, he says, "In Australia, you can live next door to people for ten years and they will hardly speak to you, never mind ask questions."

In real life 45% of Australians are foreign. Ramsay Street would be unrecognisable if scripted by Mr Treborlang. Houses would be plagued by deadly funnel web spiders; there would be a family of Brits who are permanently at war with the Robinsons, complain about the all-night parties at the Lebanese family's house, but are chummy with the Greeks next door.

As for Mrs Mangel, she would be the daughter of an Aborigine woman, which fact she would keep a close secret. Sounds more like *EastEnders*!

Kylie and Jason on their relationship...

Jason: Kylie and I are really close friends, but there's no romance. I don't have a girlfriend.

Kylie: We're good mates, but we don't really have time for anything more.

But a guest star in **Neighbours** asked Kylie for a date...and was told she was "spoken for". Who can it be?

Writers of **Neighbours** are paid just £800 an epsiode, well under what UK soap writers earn.

Kylie Minogue's sister Danielle was a star long before her big sister. She won a permanent spot on *Young Talent Time*, a popular Australian variety show, when she was just eleven years old. She's now left to take a role in *All The Way*, a lavish drama series in which she plays the daughter of an MP.

YOU MUST REMEMBER THIS . . .

Earlier this year, after **Neighbours** had first made its big breakthrough on British television, two of its stars, Kylie Minogue and Jason Donovan, both visited this country. Their presence on these shores gave English reporters a field day, and almost every day the faces of the young actor and actress were to be seen in our newspapers. Perhaps you remember some of the stories that surrounded them...

27th March. Kylie arrives and is mobbed by fans at the airport. The press however take her to task for the casual nature of her clothes and say she should smarten herself up. She is quizzed about romance with Jason and denies they are anything more than friends.

30th March. Kylie visits Harrods. However, to the disappointment of the press, buys nothing but some notepaper.

31st March. Kylie attends a charity lunch in aid of "Help a London Child". Also present are pop stars Phil Collins, Annie Lennox, Dave Stewart and Kim Wilde, as well as **Neighbours'** most famous fan, Princess Diana.

1st April. Jason flies in whilst Kylie continues to record her debut album. He too denies rumours of romance.

2nd April. Kylie is taken to task for leaving half her dinner in a posh restaurant. "Don't you know there are people starving in Africa?" says a busybody. "Name two of them," snaps back an angry Kylie.

3rd April. The two of them are seen out together in an exclusive nightclub, Browns, but leave separately. Kylie by this time has five different bodyguards!

5th April. The two stars learn of the death of their fellow actress Myra de Groot, who played Eileen in the series. Both are deeply shocked.

6th April. On BBC's *Open Air* programme, Jason fights back tears as he tells Pattie Coldwell, "She was a great lady. I am so sad."

7th April. Kylie jets out, turning the tables on the reporters as she does so by filming them with her own video camera. Jason continues discussions over a recording deal with hitmakers Stock, Aitken and Waterman.

After such a punishing schedule, the two stars must have found the long days back on the **Neighbours** set quite relaxing!

☆ STAR ☆

PROFILE

PETER
O'BRIEN
alias SHANE RAMSAY

ON HIS EARLY LIFE

"My parents were dairy farmers in Murray Bridge, South Australia. After getting my degree, I worked there as a teacher. They were a great bunch of people there, but I couldn't relate to the settled life that they wanted. I had a secure job, I'd bought a house, everyone was waiting for me to announce my engagement and I didn't even have a girlfriend. I was champing at the bit to get out. I guess I knew I didn't want to be a teacher for the rest of my life. In a place like Adelaide it's very easy to settle into a rut. A lot of people get married, have kids, and stay in the same job forever. I was always too restless for that."

ON HIS EARLY ACTING EXPERIENCE

"While I was at university in Adelaide I did a drama course. One of the teachers was also tied up with a casting agent and she suggested I do some modelling. I had always liked the idea of being an actor, but I had never seriously considered it. I couldn't afford to go to the National Institute of Dramatic Art – Australia's equivalent of RADA – but I got by the best I could. I did commercials and then auditioned for another Grundy Corporation soap, *Starting Out*. The show didn't last long – seventeen weeks – but I learned a hell of a lot about the business in that time. And I learned that I could actually do a job that would make me happy."

ON HIS ROLE AS SHANE

"In **Neighbours** there are only thirteen people in the cast, and the story revolves around just three families. That can make being a Casanova a little bit difficult. You wind up having to fall in love with any semi-eligible woman who strolls on to the set. It's not exactly the sort of thing that made Errol Flynn great."

"I'm a nomad at heart"

31

PETER O'BRIEN

ON THE SHOW'S SUCCESS

"**Neighbours** isn't high-flying, flashy drama. There's nothing visually special that makes it look out of the ordinary. It's a glorified look at day to day life, and I think it's close to home for a lot of people."

"The show can be a bit OTT sometimes – like when Danny dressed up as a gorilla to deliver gorrillagrams and managed to sabotage Des and Daphne's wedding – but no matter how excited the writers get we try to tone it down. For example, we insisted there had to be at least one happy relationship in Ramsay Street."

ON FAME AND FEMALES

"I don't get off on the star syndrome. People started comparing me and some of my friends, like Gary Sweet and Andrew Clarke, to an Australian version of the Hollywood Rat Pack. Only none of us is old enough to be a rat, so they've called us the Mouse Pack instead!"

"I've never been promiscuous, though I love girls. Most of my best friends are girls! But I don't pick up girls in nightclubs. I'm not interested in that side of fame. And girls ripping the shirt off my back or having to be prised from the hood of my car isn't my style. I get embarrassed and scared about that sort of thing. I like to keep my private life private, that's why I admire Mel Gibson so much. I'm a nomad at heart, I've been bumming round the world since I was seventeen. I've always loved travelling and living rough. To go into the bush in Australia – to get into the Outback – is no big deal."

ON HIS ROMANCE WITH CO-STAR ELAINE SMITH

No comment!

ON HIS REASONS FOR LEAVING THE SHOW

"I said I would play Shane for two years and that's what I did. There's only so much you can do to develop a character who has to be on air five nights a week, year in, year out. Frankly I felt they were starting to stretch the storylines."

ON THE FUTURE

"At present I'm happy in *Flying Doctors* but I know there's still an awful lot more to be achieved. Things have really only just started for me. In the meantime though, I want to be thought of as the boy next door. The kind of guy you could ask to look after your cats."

"Most of my best friends are girls"

THIS IS AUSTRALIA

BONDI THE BEAUTIFUL

Think of Australia and you think of sun, sea, sand — and surfing. Tanned, lean, bleached-blond young Aussies riding surfboards on high green walls of water — that's the image of Australia's 20,000 kilometres of coastline.

Think of an Australian beach — and you think of Bondi Beach. Bondi (the name means 'sound of water tumbling over rocks') grew in popularity because it is the closest beach to Sydney, Australia's largest city. But until the turn of the century the area was used for strolling and picnicking, rather than swimming. In fact, a law made it illegal for people to sea bathe between the hours of 8am and 8pm! People who liked a dip before breakfast were allowed to do so, but a bell was rung to get them out of the water before decent people were up and about...

That soon changed, and Bondi grew into a huge and popular leisure area. A Hawaiian islander called Duke Kahanamoku brought the first surfboard to Bondi in 1915, and as board design was improved and the boards became easier to ride, the sport really took off. Over the years a whole culture grew up around beach life and surfing — a culture that to many people epitomises Australia.

To millions of Australians Sydney's beach is still Bondi the Beautiful. Some three million of them flock there every summer to enjoy the sun, sea, sand — and, of course, the surfing.

The world's first organized life-saving movement was formed at Bondi Beach in 1906. Club members still patrol the beach, and over the years have saved many thousands of lives.

Surfing began hundreds of years ago in Hawaii, when islanders rode crude wooden planks. Captain Cook became the first white man to see surfboard riding when he sailed to Hawaii in 1778.

CONVICTS DOCTORS & FEUDING FAMILIES

A Guide to Australian Soaps

All over the world people watch television, and whether it's Bali or Belize, Millwall or Madrid, you can guarantee that there will be a soap opera somewhere near the top of the viewing charts. Brazil has given us *Dancing Days*, America *Dallas* and *Dynasty*, whilst Germany's *Black Forest Clinic* and France's *Chateauvallon* have as ardent a following in their own countries as such home grown soaps as *EastEnders*, *Coronation Street* and *Emmerdale Farm* do here in Britain. However, it is the Australian soaps, or "soapies" as they are referred to Down Under, that seem to have captured the imagination and affection of the British viewer to a larger degree than any of their rivals. **Neighbours**, of course, heads the list, but there are others beside, each of them dealing in its own special style with different facets of Australian life and different periods of its history. So here, for anyone not yet familiar with them, is a guide to Australian soaps, past and present.

THE SULLIVANS

This was the first of the Australian soaps to be broadcast here in Britain. Set in a small town, it follows the fortunes of the Sullivan family through the second world war and its aftermath. Other characters include army veteran Norm Baker, Maggie from the pub, Mrs Jessup, and the German family who run the corner shop. Its careful attention to period detail, its leisurely pace, and its treatment of such subjects as pacifism, the changing attitudes of women, and the dropping of the atomic bomb make it one of the more thoughtful of Australian soaps.

A COUNTRY PRACTICE

This is the most popular of all Australia's soap operas. Set in the imaginary Wandin Valley on the edge of the Outback, its cast of characters include a progressive doctor, a beautiful and independent woman vet, a policeman, a busybody spinster, and a ferocious hospital matron, whilst its storylines concern themselves with romance, relationships, and the kind of problems you would imagine would trouble a doctor, a vet, or a policeman in a small Outback town. Begun in 1981, the series is still in production.

THE YOUNG DOCTORS

This is the oldest of the Australian soaps, which is why the more fashion conscious viewer will have noticed the large number of medics sporting kipper ties and flared trousers. The first episode was made in 1976, the last one in 1981, although the series is frequently repeated both here and in Australia. Set in the Albert Memorial Hospital, its mixture of romance and melodrama is more like an American soap in format than many of its rivals. One of its chief pleasures is spotting the stars of later Aussie soaps early in their careers, their faces fresh, youthful, and vigorous above their dangling stethoscopes and rubber gloves.

SONS AND DAUGHTERS

Made from 1981-1987, in half hour episodes, this series has the most outrageous and convoluted storylines of all the soapies. Centring on the poor Palmers of Melbourne and the rich Hamiltons of Sydney, it is based on the theme of two twins, separated at birth, who meet twenty years later and, unaware of their past, fall in love. For some reason, this particular Australian soap enjoys enormous popularity in Belgium.

PRISONER: CELL BLOCK H

Made between 1978 and 1986, this soap, like **Neighbours**, *The Young Doctors*, and *Sons and Daughters*, was dreamed up by Reg Watson for the Grundy Organization. It is, in its subject matter, probably the most daring of the Australian shows to be seen here in Britain, dealing as it does with convicted murderers, bank robbers, and sadistic warders inside the walls of a women's prison. However, the show's subject matter means that it is normally broadcast late in the evening – too late, in fact, for many of the fans of **Neighbours**.

THE FLYING DOCTORS

Whilst not a soap in the strict sense of the word, being made in hour-long episodes, this series also centres on the medical profession. Like *Dallas* and *Dynasty*, it is made on film rather than videotape. Fans of the series, set in Cooper's Crossing, Victoria, will have welcomed the recent arrival of Peter O'Brien as a pilot after his long stint as Shane in **Neighbours**.

Peter O'Brien with co-star Rebecca Gibney

Neighbours SCRAPBOOK

Neighbours star Alan Dale is an old sports car fanatic. Over the years he has driven, amongst others, six Jags, an M.G.B., a Mercedes coupe, and a Morgan Roadster. Recently, however, he was forced to sell the Roadster to meet a tax demand. So maybe we should take his moans about being overworked and underpaid Down Under with a pinch of salt!

Working on **Neighbours** is no picnic. Starting at 6-30am, filming can go on for as long as 12 hours, five or six days a week. After that there's a couple of hours of learning lines for the next day's shooting. As Kylie Minogue says, "There's a lot to be said for working a 9 to 5 job!" The cast have to learn the equivalent of a feature film script every week.

When the show first started in Britain it earned itself the nickname "Cobbernation Street". Few of the executives or technicians responsible for its screening could have guessed that within six months "Cobbernation Street" would be almost as popular – and on more nights a week! – than the show that prompted its nickname.

In Northern Spain the natives like their soaps as much as anyone and many of them are dubbed into their native Basque language. One of these, *Ausokoak*, translates into English as **Neighbours**. However, the show in question is not the Australian soapie at all, but its English rival *EastEnders*!

On and off screen friends and sweethearts Kylie Minogue and Jason Donovan are no strangers to one another. The two first met nine years ago, when, both aged eleven, they played the roles of brother and sister in the Australian TV series, *Skyways*, which was set around an airport.

Neighbours SCRAP BOOK

As well as royalty, the show can count amongst its fans none other than Sir Les Patterson, Australia's self styled "hard-nosed, carpet bagging troubleshooter and high-profile elder statesman", as well as being Australian Minister for Tourism. Sir Les, (alias Barry Humphries, creator of Dame Edna) claims that his wife Lady Gwen has taken to calling their two teenage children, Craig and Karen, "Shane and Charlene", and that she has spent a small fortune redecorating their lounge to look like someone's place in **Neighbours**.

Chris Quinten of *Coronation Street* has expressed his interest in joining the **Neighbours** cast: "Maybe they could do with a garage mechanic," he suggests. Response from Grundy TV was encouraging: "We would most certainly be interested." Stay tuned! Will Hilda Ogden emigrate next and move in with Mrs Mangel?

Anne Haddy, after surviving stomach cancer, two heart attacks and bypass surgery, is now a confirmed healthy eater. She hasn't tasted red meat in ten years, never touches sugar, fat or dairy products, and won't drink tea or coffee.

Myra de Groot, who played Des Clarke's dreadful mother, was 51 when she died. Born in London, she appeared in Jewish charity concerts while a teenager, and made her professional debut in the 1950s.
  As a glamourous blonde, she had success with West End revues such as *Mr Venus* and *Pieces of Eight*, moving on to straight acting in *Ulysees in Nighttown* in 1959.
  After emigrating to Australia she developed a new TV and film career, including starring alongside Warren Mitchell in the film *Norman Loves Rose*.

STAR

P R O F I L E

38

ALAN DALE
alias JIM ROBINSON

ON LIFE BEFORE SOAPS

"In New Zealand I sold cars, which was driving me to distraction, but I had a wife and two young children to support. Later, I decided to study law. There were some home grown soaps by then, but I didn't have the ego to imagine that I could actually win the parts."

ON HIS CAREER AS A DISC JOCKEY

"I had a milk round to help pay for my studies and one day I heard a DJ making a total ass of himself on the air. I was certain I could do his job better. I went straight to the station, presented myself to the programme director and asked for the job. He ushered me into an empty studio to practise, and in no time I was being called in to fill in for the resident disc jockeys. After three months I was offered the spot of afternoon presenter on the number one radio station in Auckland."

"When I worked on Sydney radio's midnight to dawn shift I'd get home when my two sons were waking up. They'd get themselves off to school and by the time they came home I'd have woken up and done any interviews I had to arrange for the show that night."

ON HIS ROLE AS JIM ROBINSON

"When I read the character breakdown I couldn't believe my luck. It was like it was written for me. He's exactly the way I am. Like Jim, I have teenage children whom I have brought up on my own."

"I'm a strict parent"

ALAN DALE

"We are paid a pittance compared to the stars of American soaps"

ON BEING A FATHER

"I'm a strict parent, both on-screen and off. But I'm not tough. I believe children can play in the paddock, but they need to know where the fences are. It's hard being a sole parent, but it's more difficult when you're not in a regular series."

ON THE SHOW'S BRITISH SUCCESS

"I get stacks of letters from the UK, many from people who envy our nice houses, cars, clothes and sunshine."

ON WORK AND WAGES

"When you consider the long hours we work, we are paid a pittance compared to the stars of the American soaps. What bugs me is that, after punishing hours on the set, we spend our weekends doing publicity, and in many ways we know we have been exploited. People are let in to photograph us on the set and make fortunes out of their pictures."

"We hear about the success of **Neigbours** in Britain. It's interesting but it's not that great for us. We receive lots of extra letters – but no more money!"

ON HIS ROMANCE WITH TRACY PEARSON, A FORMER MISS AUSTRALIA

"We have nothing to hide, but talking about it makes me very nervous. Tracy and I are very compatible. We have a very firm relationship. I don't just like Tracy, I admire her a lot. It's too early to talk about marriage, though. We don't want to spoil things."

Neighbours star Guy Pearce was once stopped by a jealous boyfriend brandishing a knife. "I was in a shopping precinct signing autographs for some girls and when I turned round he was coming for me with a knife," he says. "I shouted out to him that I wasn't out to annoy him or provoke him or take his girl. I told him the knife suited him a hell of a lot better than it did me. Then I turned and walked away, frightened as hell, praying he wouldn't stab me in the back. Luckily, nothing happened, but I was shaking for quite a while after that."

Guy says that joining **Neighbours** has been an education. Mike's character has a violent family background, and it's prompted a vast number of youngsters to write to Guy to tell him their problems. "I've become terribly saddened by some of the fan mail," says Guy. "Until I joined **Neighbours** I'd no idea such terrible things happened."

THE
Neighbours

SEARCH A WORD

Find the Neighbours! How many of the Neighbours -words in the list below can you find in the grid? All the words are in straight lines, but they may read forwards, backwards, up, down — or even diagonally!

```
D N H E L E N D A N I E L S M Y
V A W E K R A L C S E D A X E D
Z V P F I Y C H A R L E S T O N
M O B H L A L A N F U S S E F U
N N E E N C I I E B C H I N D R
P O B O L E V P E D Y A T Y A G
Q D S E F L E Y A M U N E Y N W
L N R N L G M L R U I E R O N L
L O S A I I I Y Z N L N S U Y Y
E S M E L B O U R N E A O N U A
H A L U P B O E K I M H O G O N
C J A E X O P R E L A I N E U N
T P K E A N E O M A D G E I E E
I U R A M S A Y H I J F E L A D
M F E N E L R A H C J A N E K C
G I L O S I N N E D N A F E T S
```

ALAN	DES CLARKE	JIM ROBINSON	PAUL
ANNE	ELAINE	KEANE	PAULA
BELL	GIBBONS	KYLIE MINOGUE	RAMSAY
CHARLENE	GRUNDY (Television)	LASSITERS	SHANE
CHARLESTON	GUY	LUCY	STEFAN DENNIS
CLIVE	HELEN DANIELS	MADGE	TEN
DALE	HENRY	MELBOURNE	YOUNG
DANNY	JANE	MIKE	ZOE
DAPHNE	JASON DONOVAN	MITCHELL	

 STAR

PROFILE

ANNE HADDY

alias HELEN DANIELS

ON HER FIRST EXPERIENCE OF ACTING

"I went to Adelaide High School where my art teacher was Keith Michell. I remember playing a boy in *Androcles and the Lion*. Keith, who was always so dramatic in class, was making me up on the second night and I said, 'Mr Michell, so and so is spitting all over me'. He looked at me and said, 'My dear, ALL good actors spit'. Years later he came out to Australia with a play and Jim (my second husband) and I went backstage to see him. I said, 'You don't remember me, but you taught me art at school'. He didn't want to know!"

ON HER EARLY CAREER

"When I was twenty three I went to England with three other girls, who are still friends here in Melbourne, but was scared of working as an actress. So I worked for the Kellogg International Corporation as a stenographer. My mother wrote that people were asking what I was doing, so I went to a voice teacher. I read for her and she said, 'We must get you into the theatre'. I decided to get married instead to my first husband who came from Perth."

ON HER ILLNESS

"Ten years ago, whilst appearing in the stage play *Bodies*, I suffered a massive heart attack. It went as far as them having to bring me back with the electric shock fibrillators in hospital. Doctors told me afterwards that my heart had been badly damaged. I'm very lucky to be alive."

"I'm lucky to be alive"

43

ANNE HADDY

"The work is regular rather than rich"

ON HER ROLE AS HELEN DANIELS

"People say that I don't look old enough to be grandmother of a grown brood, but people look younger today. I have a photograph of my own grandmother and her family on her parents' thirtieth wedding anniversary. The four daughters and a son would be middle aged but look older than if they were living today."

ON THE PRESSURES OF WORK

"My husband Jim, who played the role of Douglas Blake in **Neighbours**, has a photographic memory – no trouble at all in remembering lines. I'm the complete opposite. I'm the worst learner in the world. I have to lock myself away and concentrate, slog and slog. Fortunately, in TV, scenes are isolated. I've never had a day off since taking over the role of Helen. In TV you can say, 'Do you mind if I sit down for a moment to catch my breath', but you can't do that on stage, of course."

ON FAME AND FORTUNE

"Both Jim and I have had parts in *Skippy*, *Flying Doctor*, *Prisoner: Cell Block H*, *Country Practice*, *Sons and Daughters*, and *Young Doctors*. I bet people in Britain think we must be loaded after all these years, but honestly, the work is regular rather than rich. Lorry drivers get more than soap stars in Australia. I would love a few more extra bucks like Joan Collins, but I suppose it must be a pain to take out your curlers if you want to pop down to the shop to buy something for the old man's tea."

ON THE FUTURE

"Every day, when I see the world outside and my wonderful husband, it feels good to be alive. Life has become much more interesting to me, every minute of it, and I have to nudge myself to remind myself how lucky I am."

THIS IS AUSTRALIA

THE STORY SO FAR

Australia is a vast country (the sixth largest in the world) that lies between the Indian and Pacific Oceans. Though it is three quarters the size of the whole of Europe, it has a small population — just two people to every square kilometre!

Captain Cook claimed Australia for Britain in 1770, and eighteen years later the first white settlers arrived. Most of them did not go willingly...

London's jails were dangerously overcrowded, and it was decided to ship convicts to Australia to live in penal settlements. In 1788 11 ships, 759 convicts, 211 soldiers, 30 wives and 12 children sailed into Botany Bay on the southeast coast. They set up a colony at Sydney, and slowly mastered the new, inhospitable land. Those first transported settlers played a crucial role in the country's development, building roads and towns and providing cheap labour for the farms and sheep stations that were set up.

There was a greater influx of settlers when gold was discovered in New South Wales and Victoria in the 1850s, and during the next ten years some 700,000 Europeans arrived to search for gold.

Since 1945 more than two million British people emigrated to Australia to start a new life, and most of them found their new life to be a good one. Vast herds of sheep and cattle roam the dry central plains, and meat, wool and dairy products are exported worldwide. Manufacturing and mining for gold, copper and other minerals provide most of the country's wealth.

Australia today is a successful, thriving young country that has grown in just two hundred years since those first white settlers arrived at Botany Bay.

Neighbours SCRAPBOOK

The character of Mrs Mangel was only supposed to be in the soap for three weeks. However, the interfering busybody proved so popular with fans that Mrs Mangel became one of Ramsay Street's permanent fixtures. Says Vivean Gray of her role as Mrs Mangel, "If I met her in real life I'd probably be very rude to her, then turn on my heel and walk away."

Long ago, before he enjoyed the popularity that he enjoys today, actor Peter O'Brien was taken to lunch by none other than Diana Ross. At the time, to help pay his way through his studies, Peter made use of his degree in physical education to land the job of a supervisor in an American summer camp. One of the children there was the daughter of singer Diana Ross, and this connection earned Peter an invitation to lunch in New York City from the American star.

Geoff Paine, who played the role of cheerful and eccentric Clive Gibbons, almost turned down the role when first offered it. At the time he rather looked down on acting in soaps. "I suppose at the time I was a bit too idealistic about the world of acting," he admits. "Playing a messenger in a gorilla suit might not be King Lear, but at least it pays the rent.

Neighbours SCRAPBOOK

Guy Pearce, who plays Mike from the coffee shop, was once Victoria's Teenage Body Building Champion. He won the title when he was just sixteen, and even now, five years later, he still gets a buzz from the sport. "I've let myself go a bit since working on **Neighbours**," he says, "but whenever I can I pump iron for three hours a day, six days a week. I love it. Once I start, I can't stop. I've been using my wages from the show to buy equipment to set up my own gymnasium at home."

Life before **Neighbours**...Stefan Dennis (Paul) trained as a chef; Paul Keane (Des) worked as a cleaner and a storeman; Alan Dale (Jim) was a milkman and a disc jockey; Anne Haddy (Helen) had a job as a stenographer; Anne Charleston (Madge) started out as a model; Peter O'Brien (Shane) taught surfing, parked cars and was a teacher before breaking into commercials.

Refugees from the defunct *Crossroads* were widely reported in the tabloid press to be heading Down Under to join the cast of **Neighbours**. Reg Watson, ex-producer of one and creator of the other, was clear how he felt on the matter: "I don't want any of them. Speculation that I do is complete rubbish." What, not even Benny as a replacement for Clive?

Actress Charlene Fenn (Nikki) thinks **Neighbours** is "absolute Dullsville"! Meanwhie, she's busy exercising her talents in other Aussie TV shows — as a big-hearted barmaid in a mini-series about sheep rustling, called *Dusty* (I thought leaves rustled, and sheep went 'baa'), and as a rebellious youngster in an episode of *Flying Doctors*, both to be seen in Britain. As to the future of **Neighbours**, Charlene doubts it will last as long as *The Sullivans* or *Prisoner: Cell Block H.* "I don't think it has the capacity to interest in the way of those other shows," she says. 15 million people here would disagree, Ms Fenn!

 **STAR**

P R O F I L E

ANNE CHARLESTON

alias MADGE MITCHELL

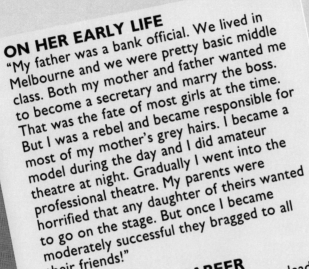

ON HER EARLY LIFE

"My father was a bank official. We lived in Melbourne and we were pretty basic middle class. Both my mother and father wanted me to become a secretary and marry the boss. That was the fate of most girls at the time. But I was a rebel and became responsible for most of my mother's grey hairs. I became a model during the day and I did amateur theatre at night. Gradually I went into the professional theatre. My parents were horrified that any daughter of theirs wanted to go on the stage. But once I became moderately successful they bragged to all their friends!"

ON HER EARLY CAREER

"I was tall and gangly and most of the leading young girl roles went to people who looked like Sandra Dee. I don't know how I managed it, but thank God, people kept putting work my way. Usually I was asked to play weeping wives or bitches or I was newly widowed! I was hired a lot because I could cry on cue but that's thanks to having weak tear ducts. I've been working for twenty seven years but it's only now, thanks to **Neighbours**, that people know who I am."

ON HER ROLE AS MADGE

"Actually Madge is a bit of a cow. She's pretty vulgar but she's a tough mum with a heart of gold somewhere underneath. I personally don't think she's the perfect mother, but the kids in Australia do – they keep voting her the country's top mum. I can certainly identify with what Madge goes through bringing a child up on her own, particularly the frustration and tiredness."

"I was a rebel"

ANNE CHARLESTON

"Madge is a bit of a cow...with a heart of gold"

ON WORK AND LEISURE

"I may go out on Friday or Saturday nights, but during the week I stay home, learn lines and get myself organized for the following day. Very often, I have to be up at five in the morning to be at the studio for six thirty. And I can't afford to include too much else in my life because I've got the home front to look after. I'm not good if I don't get eight hours sleep; I'm a disaster area."

ON MARRIAGE AND FAMILY

"I married the actor David Ravenswood when I was twenty six. We were married a couple of years but it was a total mismatch. We were just wonderful friends – and we still are, twenty years later. As well as our son, Nicholas, I adopted my cousin Suzanne's daughter, Emma, when her mother died of cancer. Suzanne and I had been like sisters so it wasn't as if I was taking on a complete stranger. It wasn't easy for her at first, but she's settled in now and calls me mum. Just looking at her happy smiling face makes it all worthwhile."

ON NEIGHBOURS' BRITISH SUCCESS

"I'm not really surprised the show has taken off in Britain. I think people like to look at the greenery and the sunshine. I knew the series was taking off when I started receiving some letters from England. I brought lots of my replies over here with me to post, because it's so much cheaper than posting from Melbourne!"

ON THE FUTURE

"I look on my role in **Neighbours** as work, and it's very basic really. I like to eat and pay the rent. Obviously, it could last, but in this business you can't depend on that and I don't get too hopeful about anything. As for marriage, I would have to be absolutely certain that it would work, otherwise there really would not be much point. There's no one special in my life right now, and I'm not unhappy with that situation."

A NEW BOY ON RAMSAY STREET

Despite his fears of being typecast in the role of – as he put it – "a slightly dim champion diver whose career is wrecked in a car crash," Peter O'Brien announced emphatically in August 1986, "I'm not leaving the show." But two months later Nine Network had made Peter an offer he couldn't refuse and he had left to join the cast of *The Flying Doctors*, which the BBC bought for screening.

However, it was not just his fans who were distressed by Peter's move between networks. The producers of **Neighbours** were left with problems of their own. Who, if anyone, could be brought into the story to replace Shane? The blonde ex-diver had been part of Ramsay Street since the show's first episode and had become, during the two years he was associated with it, one of the most popular **Neighbours** characters. Shane could be written out of the series easily enough, but who could be written in in his place?

Viewers didn't have to wait long for an answer. No sooner had they witnessed Shane's departure than it was time to welcome Henry Ramsay, Madge's son, whose existence had been kept a closely guarded secret because he was serving a jail sentence.

At first, no one was certain whether the fans would take to this new arrival. They needn't have worried, however. Soon, Henry, played by handsome newcomer Craig McClachlan, was taking not just the show, but the whole of the nation by storm. Within weeks he had become one of the most popular and familiar faces on

Australian television and now looks set to repeat that success over here in Britain.

So it's exit Shane Ramsay, enter Henry Ramsay; goodbye Peter, hello Craig. But despite all the comings and goings, the changing places and the new faces, the show rolls on and on.

DISASTER AVENUE

CHOOSE ONE PLAYER TO PUT IN JAIL

INJURED IN CAR CRASH

OVERNIGHT YOU TOTALLY CHANGE YOUR LOOKS: NO ONE NOTICES SCORE 25

YOU ARE ACCUSED OF HIGH TREASON

YOU DIE! (DONT WORRY: YOU RECOVER)

GO BACK 3

YOUR TWIN HAS YOU ARRESTED FOR IMPERSONATION

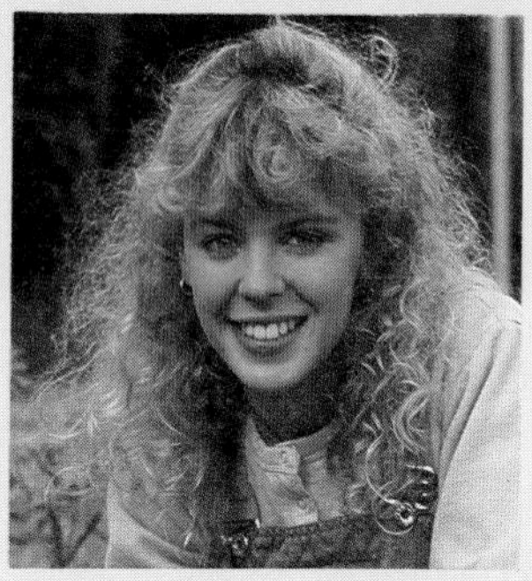

Do you want to...

GO ON 5

JET LINER CRASH LANDS ON YOUR CAR

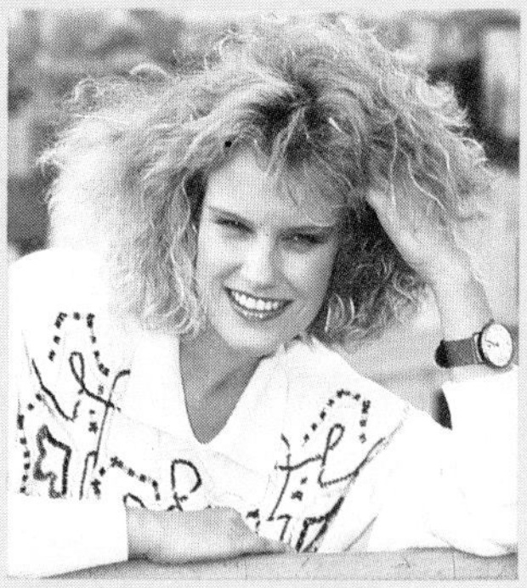

GO BACK 2

THROW A 6 FOR IMMEDIATE RELEASE

JAIL

OR MISS TWO TURNS OR PAY 10 POINTS

MYSTERY ILLNESS LANDS YOU IN HOSPITAL

- GO TO JAIL. THROW 6 TO GET OUT IMMEDIATELY OR MISS TWO TURNS OR PAY 10 POINTS.
- COLLECT POINTS TO ADD ON TO YOUR SCORE.
- GO TO HOSPITAL. THROW 6 TO RECOVER OR MISS TWO TURNS OR PAY 10 POINTS.
- GO BACK OR GO ON THE NUMBER OF SQUARES SHOWN.

GOSSIP OPTION If you can talk for one minute and make up a gossipy story involving all the other characters in the game either score 15 points or go to jail for slander if you fail.

YOUR HOUSE IS BURGLED: YOU ARE ACCUSED

YOUR ESTRANGED SPOUSE TRIES TO MURDER YOU

HARD TIMES ROAD

GOSSIP OPTION

GO ON 1

YOUR GRANDAD LEAVES YOU A LEGACY SCORE 25

YOU LAND A NEW JOB SCORE 10

YOU HAVE A BABY SCORE 15

GO BACK 4

YOUR LOST HALF-SISTER ACCUSES YOU OF PARENT BEATING

GO ON 4

YOU ARE TRODDEN ON BY AN ESCAPED ELEPHANT

GO BACK 3

YOUR HOUSE BLOWS UP IN A GAS EXPLOSION

Start ▽

FALL IN LOVE SCORE 25

GO ON 3

BEAT YOUR NEIGHBOUR?

A GAME FOR TWO OR MORE PLAYERS

Decide which character you want to play and throw to decide who starts first. Go round the board in a clockwise direction, trying to pick up points and avoid disaster.

The first player to score 200 points wins…but only if you can sing the **Neighbours** theme song all the way through (out of tune is okay).

YOUR UNCLE OFFERS YOU A NEW HOUSE SCORE 20

A FAMILY HEIRLOOM IS WORTH A FORTUNE SCORE 25

THROW A 6 FOR IMMEDIATE RECOVERY

HOSPITAL
✚

OR MISS TWO TURNS OR PAY 10 POINTS

GO ON 3

ARRESTED FOR ABDUCTING A NURSE

YOUR GREAT AUNT INVITES YOU ON A WORLD CRUISE SCORE 10

GOSSIP OPTION

YOUR AWFUL NIECE SAYS SHE'S GOING SCORE 5

GO ON 4

CHOOSE ONE PLAYER TO PUT IN HOSPITAL

 **STAR**

PROFILE

54

ELAINE SMITH

alias DAPHNE CLARKE

"I'm a very happy person"

ON HER ROLE AS DAPHNE

"The whole point of Daphne being a stripper is that she's completely counter to the black stockings and garters cliche. She's a bright girl from a good background who gets fed up with being ogled and pinched by men in her secretarial job and says, right, I might as well make some money out of it."

"Daphne wears zanier clothes than me, and she's more outgoing than I am. It's difficult because the writers are in Sydney and we're in Melbourne, but we do have our say."

ON HER EARLY LIFE

"Dad loved travelling, and we divided our lives between Australia, South Africa and Britain. Throughout school I wasn't very sports-minded so I tended to drift into drama classes. I was good at maths and my parents wanted me to be an accountant, but I decided to give acting a go because I figured if I didn't I'd regret it."

ON HER CO-STAR PETER O'BRIEN

"Just as Shane and Daphne started drifting apart on screen, Peter and I were falling in love at a pace. It's been a few years now."

ON THE BRITISH PRESS

"I'd been warned about them. They were foaming at the mouth about the stripping business. I had work convincing them I was never actually seen taking my clothes off in the series and especially not since Daphne has given all that up to run a cafe won by her garrulous grandfather in a poker game. It strikes me that perhaps those journalists hadn't actually seen the series. Still, I was pleased with the way I handled them. But I don't think I could have done it without Daphne. Daphne's confidence seems to have rubbed off on me."

ELAINE SMITH

"You have to live Neighbours twenty four hours a day"

ON THE SHOW
"Our cast has gone through lots of changes over two and a half years, but the original cast clicked straight away so it was very good. It comes across on the screen that we all like each other really, and we're just like neighbours getting fed up with each other from time to time."

"Being in **Neighbours** was fantastic at first. I made good friends. I loved having my hair done every morning. I loved the work, but you have to live **Neighbours** twenty four hours a day."

ON HER REASONS FOR LEAVING
"Daphne, the reformed stripper, was a bit of a challenge at first, but in the end, I felt trapped in her persona, never knowing how her life was going to turn out in the scriptwriter's hands."

"I kept thinking I could sit this job for years, bored but comfortable. But I had to leave because, eventually, it was no longer a challenge and there was no variety."

ON HER FUTURE
"I believe in enjoying life to its fullest and feel lucky to be in this profession. I am a very happy person. I believe in fate, so if anything goes wrong I just try to get over it as quickly as possible. In this business you have to create your own opportunities."

Neighbours

For all the millions of fans out there who find that five days a week of **Neighbours** is simply not enough to keep you going (I mean, what does a **Neighbours** fan do over the weekend?) Liverpudlian Geof Roberts has come up with the perfect answer.

Geof lived in Australia for six years, became an avid fan, and had the enviable advantage of getting to know some of the cast personally. It's handy, of course, if you happen to live round the corner from where they shoot the serial!

"When I came back from Australia," explains Geof, "people started asking me about the programme and I thought I'd help them out by setting up a fan club."

It duly started on 5th February 1988, and already boasts a membership well into the thousands, keeping Geof and his assistant well and truly busy answering over 1,000 letters a week! In conjunction with Francine Sayers, who lives in Melbourne, Geof makes sure fans are kept up to date with the latest news and photos.

"We don't give away any of the future plots," says Geof. "It only spoils it." But Geof, who keeps abreast of the serial's latest developments Down Under, tells us to keep watching. "It gets better and better!!!"

A £5 annual subscription to the fan club brings you a regular newsletter, stickers, photos, a card on your birthday, and opportunities to buy the exclusive **Neighbours** sweatshirt, as well as other special offers.

The club, which already includes MPs, professors, and clergymen along with us lesser mortals, donates 50p of every membership to the charity 'Give a Child a Chance' and 10p to 'Child Watch/Child Line', in addition to helping organizations such as the Disabled Drivers' Association and the Deaf Association.

If you'd like to join, simply send a stamped, addressed envelope to:

Mr G. L. Roberts (President),
NEIGHBOURS Fan Club (UK),
254 Liverpool Road,
Huyton,
Merseyside,
L36 3RL.

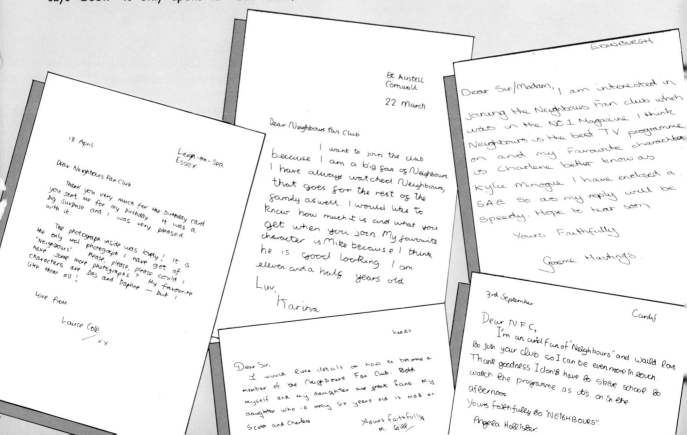

Neighbours
SCRAPBOOK

▶▶

Kylie Minogue got into acting by accident. When she was eleven years old, her sister Danielle – who now has a career of her own as a singer – was called to a TV audition. Their mum was worried that Kylie might get jealous of her sister and insisted that she come along, too. However, it turned out to be Kylie and not her sister who got the part in the show *The Sullivans*.

The residents of the close in Melbourne where the outdoor scenes for **Neighbours** are filmed are less than happy with the show's success. Flowers, fenceposts, lawn sprinklers, street signs, dustbins – in fact anything that isn't nailed down – have begun to disappear, all plundered by fans hungry for souvenirs.

Anne Charleston (Madge Mitchell) says that she was a fan of the show long before she ever dreamed she would appear in it. She says, "I was pleased to get the part because I'd become addicted to the series during three months at home as a housewife. When I saw it, I longed to appear in it myself – and my wish was granted eight weeks later."

Neighbours creator Reg Watson reckons that he gets most of his ideas for the show's storylines and new characters when he's at home gardening.

In 1988 **Neighbours** won a fistful of Logies (Australia's top TV honours) at the annual award ceremonies. The show was voted Most Popular Drama Series, and Most Popular Programme in Victoria. Kylie Minogue won the Gold Logie for Most Popular Personality on Australian TV, and a Silver Logie for Most Popular Actress. She also collected the music video award for her first single, *Locomotion*. Her friend and co-star Jason Donovan – who the year before had collected the Most Promising Newcomer Award – this year walked off with the Silver Logie for Most Popular Actor.

Even university lecturers and professional psychologists have had a go at explaining the show's phenomenal success. Says one of them, "**Neighbours** reflects a sense of community and a tempo and rhythm which matches the viewers' own lives." And we thought it was down to the sunshine, the swimming pools, and the sight of Shane or Scott in their stubbies!

Kylie Minogue once toyed with the idea of becoming a fashion designer. "I used to make a lot of my own clothes because it's a lot cheaper and you end up with something original. I still have a huge box of fabric off-cuts waiting for me to do something wonderful with."

Original titles considered for the show were *One Way Street* and *No Through Road*. No way, Bruce!

Composer Tony Hatch, who wrote the catchy **Neighbours** theme tune, earns £300 *every* week from the royalties. Members of the cast receive £700 a week. Sounds like Tony knows which side *his* bread is buttered!

It's incredible that Peter O'Brien is still in one piece. As an Australian Rules footballer he crushed a foot, smashed both shoulders, broke more fingers that he can remember, and almost lost the sight in one eye! Mind you, what's left of him is still looking pretty good, isn't it girls?

Kylie Minogue says that her dream date wouldn't be either Jason or his on-screen character Scott Robinson but, believe it or not, Fred Astaire. "I can just imagine myself in one of those long evening dresses with Fred looking immaculate in his white tie and tails. I would just have to propose to him as he whirled me round the dance floor. It would be so romantic."

THE RAMSAY STREET

You think you know all there is to know about Australia's favourite show and its cast of characters? Here's a chance to prove it. Fifty questions, some simple, some not so simple, on the soapie that's taken Britain by storm. So, get ready to test your memory in...

THE RAMSAY STREET MASTERMIND QUIZ

1 What was Kylie Minogue's number one hit in the Australian charts for seven weeks? (Clue: It was her first single.)

2 Shane Ramsay was a previous champion at which sport?

3 and 4 The character of Lucy Robinson has been played by two different actresses. Name them both.

5 The theme tunes to *Crossroads* and **Neighbours** were both written by the same composer. Name him.

6 Who sings the theme to the Australian soap?

7 Which **Neighbours** star is a fan of vintage sports cars?

8 What is his on-screen character called?

9 Who are the hitmakers responsible for *I Should Be So Lucky* and Kylie Minogue's first album?

10 What was the name of the actor who first portrayed Scott Robinson?

11 Which actor left **Neighbours** for *The Flying Doctors*?

12 Name his screen idol and fellow Australian actor whose success he is keen to emulate.

13 Which actress has played a kindhearted busybody in both **Neighbours** and, before that, *The Sullivans*?

14 What was the character who was engaged to Shane Ramsay?

15 Who did she finally marry?

16 Who, dressed as a gorilla, almost sabotaged the wedding by kidnapping the groom?

17 Which British actress, who played the part of Eileen Clarke, died in 1988?

18 On what Australian show did both Kylie Minogue and Jason Donovan make their first screen appearances?

19 What is the name of the creator of **Neighbours**?

20 What is the name of the pub in the series?

21 What was Daphne Clarke's original profession?

22 What makes **Neighbours** special to English TV?

23 Which of Clive's relatives discovered the truth about Clive's fake marriage to Susan?

24 What is the name of Helen Robinson's business?

25 When was the show first broadcast in Britain?

26 Which of the Robinsons has become a ruthless businessman?

27 How much does an episode of **Neighbours** cost to produce?

MASTERMIND QUIZ

28 Which **Neighbours** actress played Rosie in *Sons and Daughters*?

29 Which **Neighbours** actress spent the first eighteen months of her life in Largs in Scotland?

30 Who plays Charlene's screen mum?

31 The word Kylie comes from the Aborigine language. What does it mean?

32 In which other Australian soap did **Neighbours** star Alan Dale appear?

33 Which **Neighbours** star worked as, amongst other things, a supervisor at an American Summer Camp and a surfing instructor?

34 Which British pop star turned down an offer to make a guest appearance on the show?

35 What is the name of Kylie Minogue's sister?

36 What is the name of the Australian TV awards won by the show and its stars?

37 What job on the council did Jack Ramsay hold twice?

38 What other Aussie TV show did Peter O'Brien join after **Neighbours**?

39 What was the name of the bank manager Julie Robinson fell in love with?

40 How many episodes of **Neighbours** were made for Channel 7?

41 What caused the cappuccino machine to stop working in the coffee shop?

42 What number house do the Ramsays live at?

43 Name the dog the Robinsons saved after a road accident.

44 Which company first employed Shane as a chauffeur?

45 What is the name of Jim Robinson's much travelled mother?

46 Which character does Charlene Fenn play?

47 What is Kylie Minogue's middle name?

48 When Danny and Scott ran away who did they stay with?

49 Who first talked Helen into exhibiting her paintings?

50 Which city is **Neighbours** set in?

RATING

Under 15: You've been watching too much *EastEnders*.

15–24: You must have just discovered **Neighbours**.

25–34: Clearly a dedicated fan!

35–44: They make medals for people like you...

45–50: You must be one of the cast.

QUIZ ANSWERS

1	*The Locomotion*	26	Paul
2	Diving	27	£20,000
3	Kylie Flinker	28	Anne Haddy
4	Sacha Close	29	Elaine Smith
5	Tony Hatch	30	Anne Charleston
6	Barry Crocker	31	Boomerang
7	Alan Dale	32	*The Young Doctors*
8	Jim Robinson	33	Peter O'Brien
9	Stock, Aitken and Waterman	34	George Michael
10	Darius Perkins	35	Danielle
11	Peter O'Brien	36	The Logies
12	Mel Gibson	37	Mayor
13	Vivean Gray	38	*The Flying Doctors*
14	Daphne Clarke	39	Philip Martin
15	Des	40	170
16	Clive Gibbons	41	A lucky sixpence
17	Myra de Groot	42	No. 24
18	*Skyways*	43	Patch
19	Reg Watson	44	Fielding Enterprises
20	The Waterhole	45	Bess
21	A stripper	46	Nikki Dennison
22	It's the only TV soap broadcast five days a week	47	Ann
23	Uncle Ted	48	Mrs Forbes
24	Home James	49	Des Clarke
25	November 1986	50	Melbourne